SCHOLASTIC

100 Awesome Writing Prompts
to Use With Any Book!

LIZA CHARLESWORTH

New York • Toronto • London • Auckland • Sydney •
New Delhi • Mexico City • Hong Kong • Buenos Aires

Teaching Resources

DEDICATION

To the writers of the world,
who inspire us to read and dream...

Writing samples by Adriane Rozier
Cover design by Maria Lilja
Cover illustration and interior illustrations by Jared Lee
Interior design by Grafica, Inc.

ISBN-13: 978-0-439-22723-0
ISBN-10: 0-439-22723-2

2 3 4 5 6 7 8 9 10   40   17 16 15 14 13 12 11 10

TABLE OF CONTENTS

INTRODUCTION

ew pleasures compare to cracking open a book and getting lost in its pages. Whether they are indulging in a heart-pounding adventure located in icy Alaska, a gripping mystery about a missing sarcophagus, or a tale of abiding friendship set against the backdrop of the Civil War, reading transports kids to other worlds and actively engages their minds and spirits. But as important as the act of reading is, it's also essential—in this day of assessment and testing—that students possess the ability to carefully reflect upon and effectively write about the books they read.

That's where *100 Awesome Writing Prompts to Use With Any Book!* comes in. It offers dozens of kid-pleasing activities sure to take the groans out of journal writing or rote response questions. These 10- to 20-minute prompts and lively graphic organizers are specially designed to truly engage children of all learning styles and strengths. Each time you assign one, you'll help students learn to sort and classify information, build comprehension, develop critical-thinking skills, and internalize must-know literary elements including character, plot, setting, genre, and style. You'll also help kids strengthen their own writing skills through meaningful practice. And, when children are able readers and writers, they are well equipped to be successful learners—both in and out of the classroom.

How To Use This Book

Incorporating the Prompts Into Your Reading Program

This resource has been designed for flexible use. These quick and fun prompts and graphic organizers can be used in conjunction with any book to enrich kids' understanding of the story and encourage thoughtful writing. Present the activities at a specified time of the day or whenever the mood strikes. They're a great follow-up to independent reading, make perfect seatwork for those times you work with small groups, and are a welcome alternative to ho-hum homework assignments. They're also perfect for:

- Daily journals
- Literature logs
- Writing centers
- Literature-circle conversation starters
- Creative alternatives to book reports
- Focused prep for writing assessments and standardized tests

Incorporating these prompts into your classroom practice will develop the following:

- Reading Comprehension
- Critical Thinking
- Creative Thinking
- Communication
- Writing
- Story Structure
- Plot
- Character
- Setting
- Genre
- Style
- Vocabulary
- Sorting and Classifying Data
- Comparing Texts
- Connecting Story With Students' Lives

Presenting the Prompts

Because all 100 prompts were developed to use with any book, you can confidently choose one to share with the entire class—even if students are reading an array of genres at vastly different levels. Present each activity by jotting it on the board, copying it onto a transparency for an overhead projector, or inviting individual students to peruse the book and make their own selections. **TIP:** Create a set of durable reader-response cards by photocopying each page onto heavy paper, cutting out the prompts along the lines, laminating them, and placing a complete set in an accessible recipe box.

Building Skills With Specific Prompts

If a child, group, or your whole class is having trouble grasping a particular literary element, such as identifying the theme of a story, select a fitting prompt—such as "Big Idea Bulb" (page 30) or "Message in a Bottle" (page 33)—to help the student or students explore the topic through example and writing. **TIP:** If you like, present a mini-lesson of your own design beforehand to help frame the skill.

CARD #1

What an Animal!

If the main character of your book were an animal, what do you figure he or she would be? A proud peacock, a noble dolphin, a fiendish crocodile, a sneaky raccoon? Think about that character's traits and personality, then tell how he or she is like the creature you chose. Don't be afraid to let your imagination run wild!

CARD #2

Totally Terrific Tongue Twisters

Make up a marvelous tongue twister that tells all about a character in your book. Bet you can't say it ten times fast!

★ **BONUS** —————————————————————
For an extra challenge, try making up a different tongue twister for each of the major characters in your book.

The big bad wolf wanted bacon badly but only got badly burned. Boo-hoo!

CARD #3

Character

Alphabet "Scoop"

There's nothing like a steaming bowl of alphabet soup to get the scoop on a character! Copy the soup bowl onto a sheet of paper, then fill it with at least ten words that best describe his or her personality. When you're finished, share your "souper" list with some classmates who've read the same book and see if they can guess the person that you've described.

mean   homely   sneaky
dishonest   scary
dangerous
skinny   jealous   angry
hot-tempered

Wicked Witch of the West

The Wizard of Oz by L. Frank Baum

CARD #4

Character

Conversation Hearts

Quick! Pick one of the candy hearts below. Then challenge yourself to write a paragraph telling how it relates to a character in your book.

Always

Magic

Sweet & Sour

Awesome

Kind Heart

No

Think Fast

Double Trouble

Smartie

Yes

So Shy

Maybe

True Love

Surprise!

CARD #5 Character

Guess Who's Coming to Dinner

You're having a fancy dinner party and you've invited a character from the book you are reading *plus* another character from a totally different book. Tell which characters you would choose (and what books they are from). Then write a mini-story about what happens during the meal. Do the two become fast friends and forget all about you? Or does one end up dumping a tossed salad on the other's head? Use their personality traits to create a meeting that makes sense...but don't be afraid to have fun!

CARD #6 Character

Character Haikus

A haiku is an ancient form of Japanese poetry that paints a meaningful picture in just a few words. The first line has five syllables, the second line has seven, and the third line again has five. Challenge yourself to create descriptive haikus for three or more of the characters in your book. After you're done, share your mini-masterpieces with some friends who've read the same book and see if they can guess who's the star of each one.

Stuart Little

Tiny, furry, kind,
The rodent in the roadster
With a great big heart

Encyclopedia Brown

Smart boy, not a clown,
This super-duper young sleuth
Finds bad guys in town

CARD #7

Desert Island Top-Ten List

Pretend one of the main characters in your book is going to spend a yearlong vacation alone on a desert island. Doesn't sound like much fun, huh? Well, you can make his or her stay more pleasant—and less lonely—by helping that character pack ten meaningful objects from home. Make a list of what you would choose, and don't forget to tell why.

Things to Pack for Laura Ingalls' Trip

1. Pa's fiddle because she loves it more than anything

2. A gingham sunbonnet to keep her from getting sunburned and to remind her of the prairie

3. Paper, ink, and a quill pen so she can write down all her adventures

CARD #8

Ups and Downs

Q. How is a person's life like a seesaw? **A.** It's sure to be filled with plenty of ups and downs! What ups and downs has the main character in your story experienced? Copy the seesaw graphic organizer onto a sheet of paper. Then fill in that character's high points and low points. When you're finished, choose one of those events and write about how it changed him or her for better or worse.

UPS

1. Sara was rich and had the best room in school.
2. Sara was popular and had many friends.
3. Sara loved her father and he loved her.

1. Sara's father died and lost their money.
2. Sara had to live in the attic and work for the school.
3. Sara was cold and hungry and Lavinia was mean to her.

DOWNS

Sara Crewe

A Little Princess
by Frances Hodgson Burnett

© 2010 by Liza Charlesworth, Scholastic Teaching Resources

CARD #9

Dear Pen Pal

One of the main characters in your book has just joined a pen-pal club and is writing his or her very first letter to a total stranger, who lives clear across the country. Pretend you *are* that character and write an introductory letter that tells all about yourself, including your personality, likes and dislikes, problems, family situation, hobbies, appearance, and whatever else your new friend will need to know to get the inside scoop on you.

CARD #10

Character Crystal Ball

What do you predict will happen to a favorite character beyond the pages of your book? What has he or she learned? How has he or she changed? Draw a crystal ball like the one at the right. Then write one or more important things that you think will happen to that character in the future.

⭐ BONUS ⭐
For an extra challenge, make a prediction for each of the important characters in your book.

1. She will go to the woods with an adult.
2. She will have trouble falling asleep at night.
3. She will always be nice to bears!

Goldilocks

CARD #11

Meeting of the Minds

If a character from your book were able to climb inside a time machine and zoom backward—or forward—in time to meet a famous person, who would it be? George Washington? Amelia Earhart? Jackie Robinson? Use your imagination and tell who you would choose and what that says about the character's personality. What do you think the meeting would be like? Set the scene in writing.

⭐**BONUS** ....

For an extra challenge, write a make-believe mini-dialogue of what the two would say to each other.

CARD #12

"T" Time

Most people—and characters—have a combination of traits we admire and traits we don't admire. For instance, they might be incredibly brave, but selfish at the same time. Choose a character from your book that you have mixed feelings about. Then use a T-chart like this one to list things you like about him or her on the left, and things you don't like on the right. Is this someone you'd choose to have as a friend? Tell why or why not.

Little Women by Louisa May Alcott

Jo March

Like	Dislike
1. Brave	1. Bossy
2. A good writer	2. Impulsive
3. Loyal	3. Bad temper
4. Smart	4. Competitive

CARD #13

Cooking Up a Character

What ingredients combine to make a character from your book truly memorable? A fresh outlook on life? A heaping cup of humor? Two tablespoons of courage? A pinch of prankishness? Use the model to the right and an index card to whip up a fantasy recipe that describes the personality of your character to a tee. Be sure to include appropriate ingredients and cooking directions. Tap your imagination and get creative!

Holes by Louis Sachar:
Stanley Yelnats Survival Soufflé

- 2 cups of hard work
- A hint of humor and lots of honesty
- A pinch of perseverance
- A big bowl of family history

To Make:

First mix your two cups of hard work. When you get discouraged, add a hint of humor and lots of honesty. Sift the honesty, hard work, and humor into a big bowl of family history. Study the history carefully before putting the mixture in the oven. Sprinkle on a bit of perseverance before baking.

CARD #14

Trophy Tribute

If you were going to give a character in your book a great big trophy, what would it be for? Maintaining a super sense of humor? Never ever giving up? Being the klutziest kid in America? Think about what makes a character in your book outstanding or unique. Then tell what you would inscribe on a "loving cup" (special trophy) to honor him or her. Be serious or silly—it's up to you!

Awarded to the kindest, wisest, most thoughtful, loving, helpful, and insightful grandmother in the world!

ABUELITA

Felita
by Nicholasa Mohr

CARD #15

Candid Camera

It's said that beauty is only skin-deep. Still, a character's looks can provide important clues to his or her personality. Browse through your book and make a list of phrases that describe the main character's physical appearance. Now close your eyes and pretend you are staring at a snapshot of this person. What do you see? Spiky red hair? Purple hightops? A kid slumped at the kitchen table staring at a cereal bowl? Use your imagination to write a picture-perfect description that freezes the character in time and captures something about his or her personality.

⭐ BONUS ··

If you're feeling artistic, draw the picture too!

CARD #16

Incredible Quotations

The things that characters say are like keys that help readers unlock their personalities. Search through your book and see if you can find a quote that fits the bill for each category to the right. Be sure to include the name of the speaker and a sentence that tells why you chose it.

To be or not to be, that is the question.

1 A quote that revealed something important about the speaker

2 A quote that made you mad

3 A quote that made you laugh

4 A quote that surprised you

5 A quote that made you think

100 Awesome Writing Prompts to Use With Any Book! © 2010 by Liza Charlesworth, Scholastic Teaching Resources

CARD #17

Bottle It!

Have you ever seen a ship inside a bottle and wondered, "How did they do that?" Well, now it's your turn to amaze friends—and your teacher—by getting a whole setting inside one! Copy the bottle shape onto a sheet of paper. Then fill it with a paragraph that describes a key setting from your book. Be sure to include as much detail as possible.

Brian crashes near a lake. The lake is surrounded by forest, green pine and spruce trees. There is small brush growing close to the ground, and in the distance are low rocky hills. Across the lake is a beaver lodge with beavers swimming around it. The forest is full of the sounds of wildlife. Birds sing and fish splash.

Hatchet by Gary Paulsen

CARD #18

Awesome Acrostics

Where does your story take place? Alaska? The Land of Oz? Brad's bedroom? Choose an important setting in your book and write it down the left side of a piece of paper as shown. Next, use those letters as starting points to describe that very special place in words and phrases. Hey! You're a poet...and you didn't even know it!

Setting from **Julie of the Wolves**
by Jean Craighead George
A place for brave people who
Love nature and wolves
And are good at building ice houses.
So cold it's hard to survive. Better
Keep a dogsled to get around.
Alaska is amazing!

CARD #19

Worlds Within Worlds

Most of the books we read take us to worlds within worlds. What does that mean? Well, a story might be set in a treehouse, which is set in a backyard, which is set in a neighborhood, which is set in a town, which is set in a state, which is set in a country, which is set on the planet Earth, which is set in the universe... Wow, what a journey! On a sheet of paper, draw a graphic organizer like the one at right. Then use your book as reference to fill in as many worlds within worlds as you can.

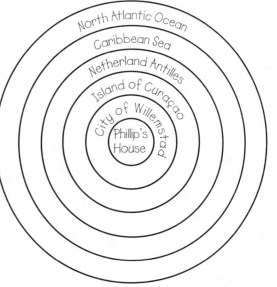

North Atlantic Ocean
Caribbean Sea
Netherland Antilles
Island of Curaçao
City of Willemstad
Phillip's House

The Cay by Theodore Taylor

CARD #20

Make a Map

Well-written books help us see pictures in our minds. Think of an important setting in your book and use your imagination to draw a map of what you think it looks like. It might be a whole town, a magic forest, or even the inside of a character's shoe! Be sure to include labels and a map key. You don't want folks to get lost, do you?

CARD #21

Listing Locations

Some books have one main setting. Others have lots and lots. For example, a story might be set in a character's home and his school and a haunted house and his best friend's room and a baseball field and a mall... Okay, I think you get the idea. Look through your book and make a list of every setting you can find. When you're finished, get together with your classmates who read other books. Compare lists. Whose book had the most settings? Whose had the least?

CARD #22

Inside-Out

Most books have a combination of indoor and outdoor settings, such as a character's attic and her backyard. Copy a graphic organizer like the one here onto a sheet of paper. First choose an important indoor setting and write a paragraph to describe it *inside* the box. Second, choose an important outside setting and write a paragraph that describes it *outside* the box. Which place do you prefer? Tell why.

Indoor	Outdoor
The witch's house is dark, musty, cold, and lonely. The floor is made of stone.	The forest is green and smells of pine. Birds sing and animals chatter.

Hansel and Gretel

CARD #23

Prized Setting

The book you read probably took place in a lot of different locations, but which one did you like best of all? Copy this first-prize ribbon onto a sheet of paper. Then award it to the #1 setting in your book. Why did you pick it? Did the place create a beautiful picture in your mind? Was it essential to the plot? Did it remind you of a spot you love? Explain your answer in writing.

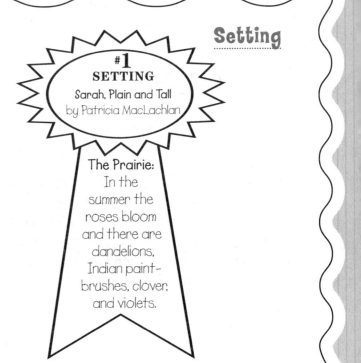

<u>Setting</u>

#1 SETTING
Sarah, Plain and Tall
by Patricia MacLachlan

The Prairie:
In the summer the roses bloom and there are dandelions, Indian paint-brushes, clover, and violets.

CARD #24

Place Postcard

Create a cool postcard that celebrates a favorite setting from your book. It could be a rain-forest, an ice-cream parlor, or even the dust-bunny infested land underneath a character's bed! Start with a blank index card. On one side, draw a picture of the place and write *Greetings from…* _____ (setting). On the other side, pre-tend you just vacationed there and are anxious to tell a friend all about it. When you're done, address and "mail" it to a classmate who *hasn't* read the book. Does the postcard whet his or her appetite to journey into its pages?

<u>Setting</u>

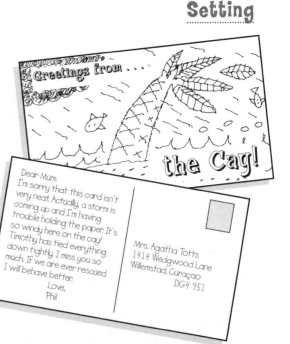

Greetings from . . . . the Cay!

Dear Mum:
I'm sorry that this card isn't very neat. Actually, a storm is coming up and I'm having trouble holding the paper. It's so windy here on the cay! Timothy has tied everything down tightly. I miss you so much. If we are ever rescued I will behave better.
Love,
Phil

Mrs. Agatha Totts
1414 Wedgwood Lane
Willemstad, Curaçao
DG4 951

CARD #25

Set Design

Lucky you! A Broadway producer is turning the book you just read into a play, and she's hired you to be the set designer. Choose a favorite scene from the story and write a detailed plan telling how you'll set up the stage. Is there a backdrop of skyscrapers? A park bench near a statue of George Washington? A banana peel waiting to be slipped on? Use your book and your imagination as references to get every detail. Don't let your audience down!

BONUS ⋯⋯⋯⋯⋯⋯⋯⋯⋯⋯⋯⋯⋯⋯⋯⋯⋯⋯⋯⋯⋯⋯⋯⋯⋯⋯⋯⋯⋯⋯

If you're feeling artistic, draw the set, too.

CARD #26

Frame That Place

What do great artists and writers have in common? Both have the ability to bring settings to life. Choose a favorite setting in your book. Copy these two frames onto a sheet of paper. In one, use your pencil, markers, or crayons to create a perfect picture of that special spot. In the other, use words to write a careful description. When you're finished, share both "artworks" with classmates who've read the book. Which do they think better captures that incredible location?

Draw   **Write**

Claudia and Jamie slept on a beautiful 16th-century bed. It was high up and had a canopy. It had two big posts on either side of the carved headboard. It also had draperies that you can close.

From the Mixed-Up Files of Mrs. Basil E. Frankweiler by E. L. Konigsburg

CARD #27

More, More, More

I s there a setting in your book that disappointed you because its description was too short or vague? Find it and use your mind's eye and imagination to flesh it out in writing. Don't be afraid to get super-duper detailed. When you're finished, try your new, improved description out on a friend who's read the book. Do they feel more satisfied?

CARD #28

Their Place, Your Place

A s readers we sometimes have special connections with certain settings because they remind us of places in our own world. A scene set in a clubhouse, for example, might trigger thoughts of a secret hideaway you share with friends. Is there a place like that in the book you just read? Copy the Venn diagram onto a sheet of paper. In the circle on the right, write words that describe a spot from your book. In the circle on the left, write words that describe a spot from your life. In the center, write words that describe both.

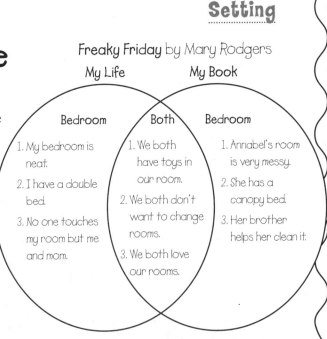

Freaky Friday by Mary Rodgers

My Life   My Book

Bedroom   Both   Bedroom

1. My bedroom is neat.
2. I have a double bed.
3. No one touches my room but me and mom.

1. We both have toys in our room.
2. We both don't want to change rooms.
3. We both love our rooms.

1. Annabel's room is very messy.
2. She has a canopy bed.
3. Her brother helps her clean it.

100 Awesome Writing Prompts to Use With Any Book! © 2010 by Liza Charlesworth, Scholastic Teaching Resources

CARD #29

It Happened Here

Where did the most important part of your book's plot take place? A classroom? A haunted mansion? Up a tree? Pick the single most important scene in your book and describe its setting in detail. How did the location help to build the story's drama? Why do you think the author chose it?

CARD #30

Setting Scavenger Hunt

Some books keep the reader interested—and moving!—by presenting lots and lots of diverse settings. Is your book like that? Hunt through its pages and see if you can find a scene that fits each category. Be sure to explain your choices with a sentence or two. (**Hint:** If you like, you can use a setting more than once.)

- A place the main character likes
- A place the main character doesn't like
- A surprising place
- A spooky place
- A funny place
- A crowded place
- A quiet place
- A beautiful place
- A place where the most important part of the plot took place
- A place that made you think

CARD #31

Dear Blabby

Pretend a character in your book has written a "Dear Blabby" letter to a newspaper columnist asking for advice with a BIG problem. What would it be? Put yourself in his or her shoes and write it. Now put yourself in Blabby's shoes and craft a thoughtful response to help that character come up with a solid solution.

CARD #32

Lights, Camera, Action!

Hollywood wants you to turn the book you just read into a movie! There's only once catch: you're on a tight budget and don't have much film. Copy the movie graphic organizer onto a sheet of paper. Fill the first frame with a mini-description of the beginning of the story; fill the second frame with a mini-description of the middle; fill the last frame with a mini-description of the end. Be brief, but don't leave anything important on the cutting-room floor.

Beginning	Middle	End

CARD #33

Step Into the Story

Think of *plot* as a staircase full of steps leading up, up, up to your book's conclusion. Copy the staircase graphic organizer onto a sheet of paper. Then write a key event on each step until you reach the end of the story. (**Hint:** Draw as many steps as you need.) For an extra challenge, write about which "step" is the most important to the story and why.

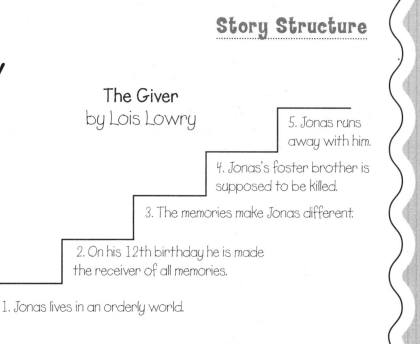

The Giver
by Lois Lowry

5. Jonas runs away with him.

4. Jonas's foster brother is supposed to be killed.

3. The memories make Jonas different.

2. On his 12th birthday he is made the receiver of all memories.

1. Jonas lives in an orderly world.

CARD #34

Extra! Extra!

You're an ace reporter who's just been handed a plum assignment: retell the plot of the book you just read in the form of a nonfiction newspaper article. Be sure to stick to the facts and include answers to these six key questions: *Who? What? Where? When? Why? How?* When your article is complete, give it an attention-grabbing headline like "Girl With 300-foot-long Hair Escapes Tower and Weds Local Prince" (for *Rapunzel).*

CARD #35

Fairy-Tale Retelling

Starting with "Once upon a time," retell the book you just read in the form of a teeny-weeny fairy tale. Does it end "happily ever after"?

nce upon a time there was a girl who dreamed of the day her real mother would come to rescue her...

The Great Gilly Hopkins
by Katherine Paterson

CARD #36

Ten-Event Timeline

Can you retell the story you just read in ten events? Give it a try! Create a cool timeline that highlights the ten most important happenings in your book. Which ones have to be included? Which ones won't make the cut? If you like, add cool pictures (either drawn or clipped from magazines) to make your timeline extra snazzy!

Bud, Not Buddy by Christopher Paul Curtis

Bud goes to a new foster home.	Bud gets beat up and runs away.	Bud has breakfast with a pretend family.	Bud reads at the library.	Bud tries to hop a freight train.
1	2	3	4	5

Bud decides to walk to Grand Rapids.	Lefty meets Bud and drives him to Grand Rapids.	Bud meets Herman E. Calloway.	Bud discovers Herman is his grandfather.	Bud gets an instrument and stays with his grandfather.
6	7	8	9	10

100 Awesome Writing Prompts to Use With Any Book! © 2010 by Liza Charlesworth, Scholastic Teaching Resources

CARD #37

Story Structure

Radio Play

Turn a favorite scene in your book into a short radio play. How? First convert the scene into a script with dialogue for all of the main characters plus a narrator to communicate nonverbal action. Then cast friends in the key roles, practice until it's perfect, and record it on a tape recorder complete with music and sound effects. Voilá! You've created a radio play to share with your class. Bet they'll be on the edge of their seats!

It was a dark and stormy afternoon...

CARD #38

Story Structure

Conflict Cartoon

Every story has at least one conflict (or "problem"). Take "The Three Little Pigs," for example. If the Big Bad Wolf didn't attempt to eat those little pigs, there'd be nothing to tell, right? Now think about the book you just read and try to determine the main conflict. When you've got it, create a cartoon strip that presents the problem and the resolution.

BONUS
For an extra challenge, write about the resolution. Was it a happy one? Did it satisfy you? Why or why not?

CARD #39

Incredible Cliffhangers

Did a chapter in your book end with such an incredible cliff-hanger that you just *had* to read on? If so, the author achieved his or her goal of getting you to sweat a little...and quickly turn the page. Copy the cliff-hanger graphic organizer onto a sheet of paper. Write the big problem that had you on pins and needles at the edge of the "cliff." Then write the resolution on the "parachute." Were you happy with how things turned out? Put your opinion in a paragraph.

Hatchet by Gary Paulsen

Problem	Solution
When Brian's plane crashes in the Canadian wilderness, he has no food.	Brian follows birds to some berry trees. Then he eats the berries and stays alive.

CARD #40

Retooling the Title

Now that you've finished reading your book, how do you feel about its title? Is it right on target? Does it provide a valuable clue to the story line? Tell why you do or don't think so. Then tap your imagination and come up with an alternative title of your own. Be sure to tell why you feel it really fits the bill. For an extra challenge, redesign the cover with great new artwork to showcase your great new title.

100 Awesome Writing Prompts to Use With Any Book! © 2010 by Liza Charlesworth, Scholastic Teaching Resources

CARD #41

Changing Chapter Titles

Does the book you just read have descriptive chapter titles (like "The Frantic Friday Morning Math Quiz") or just plain-old numbers (like "Chapter 9")? Either way, take this challenge: see if you can concoct brand-new names for each chapter that grab the reader and communicate the content (without giving too much away, of course). Make a chart like the one at right. Write the old chapter names—or numbers— down the left side and your new, improved ones on the right.

How to Eat Fried Worms
by Thomas Rockwell

Old Chapter Titles	New Chapter Titles
Out of the Frying Pan and Into the Oven	Trouble!
Pearl Harbor	A Sneak Attack
$%#! Blip *+&!	It Ain't Over 'til It's Over

CARD #42

Story Rap

Calling all rap stars! Can you retell the plot of your book in a hip-hop rhyme of your own design? Give it a try. For added fun, capture your stylings with an audio recording. Your classmates won't want to miss your funky, fresh performance!

THE PLOT THICKENS

CARD #43

Find That Feeling

The great thing about a book is that it can make the reader laugh, cry, get mad, scared, feel worried—then relieved and joyful...and that's just in the first 50 pages! Browse through the book you just read and see if you can find a scene that made you feel each of the emotions listed at right. Write them down. Then discuss your findings with a classmate who's read the same story and done the assignment. Were some of his or her answers different from yours?

Find the scenes that made you feel...

1. Happy	6. Relieved
2. Sad	7. Like laughing
3. Worried	8. Surprised
4. Frightened	9. Confused
5. Angry	

CARD #44

Key Event

What is the single most important event in the book you just read? A boy hitting a grand slam? A girl coming down with a case of scarlet fever?

Tuck Everlasting by Natalie Babbitt

The key event of this story is when Winnie sees Jesse Tuck drink the water in the woods.

A smart fish choosing to attend a new "school"? Copy the key graphic organizer onto a sheet of paper. Then fill it with a description of what you consider to be the story's key event. Be sure to explain in writing why you think it fits the bill.

100 Awesome Writing Prompts to Use With Any Book! © 2010 by Liza Charlesworth, Scholastic Teaching Resources

CARD #45

Add a Chapter

When you've finished the very last page of a great story, do you ever find yourself thinking, "I wonder what happened next"? Think carefully about the book you just read, kick your imagination into high gear, and tell what you think would occur in the following chapter...if there were a following chapter, that is. When you've completed the assignment, compare your ending with classmates who've read the same book. Which version is the most fun? Which makes the most sense? Write all about it!

CARD #46

Cause-and-Effect Kaboom!

Kaboom! Think of *cause* as a stick of dynamite and *effect* as the explosion it creates. An example of *cause* is Sleeping Beauty pricking her finger on the spinning wheel; an example of *effect* is Sleeping Beauty falling asleep for 100 years. Browse through your book and locate a cause that brought about a powerful effect. (It can be a good effect or a bad effect.) When you find one, copy the graphic organizer at right onto a sheet of paper and fill it in.

CAUSE
The Maldonados' new neighbors were mean, hurting Felita and her brother.

EFFECT
Felita's parents decide to move back to the old neighborhood.

Felita by Nicholasa Mohr

CARD #47

Big-Idea Bulb

Quick! What's the BIG idea of the story you just read? Copy the light-bulb graphic organizer onto a sheet of paper and fill it with a sentence that communicates what you think is the book's most important message. Does that message relate to your own life? Use brain power to write a paragraph telling why it does or doesn't.

It's important to be true to your family inside, no matter how other people treat you.

Roll of Thunder, Hear My Cry
by Mildred D. Taylor

CARD #48

In a Word

If you had to describe the theme—or message—of the book you just read in a single word, what would it be: Courage? Humor? Change? Challenge yourself to find the one word that best captures it. Then write a paragraph explaining your choice. When you're done, compare words with classmates who've read the same book.

Truth   FAME

JEALOUSY   Love

Kindness

Betrayal

HONOR

Journey

100 Awesome Writing Prompts to Use With Any Book! © 2010 by Liza Charlesworth, Scholastic Teaching Resources

CARD #49

Story Quilt

Theme

Good books teach us things and make us think. What did you learn from the story you just read? Copy the nine-patch quilt onto a sheet of paper. Now fill each square with a different thing the book taught you. It could be a fact (like "Spiders have eight legs.") or an opinion (like "Kids should respect their grandparents.")

★ BONUS ....
For an extra challenge, choose the square that you think is the most important and write a paragraph explaining why.

Holes by Louis Sachar

1. Keep your promises.	2. Don't judge people by their outsides.	3. Know your family history.
4. Stick by your friends.	5. Don't take advantage of nice people.	6. Work hard!
7. Never give up.	8. What goes around, comes around.	9. Choose your friends wisely.

CARD #50

"Reigning" Messages

Theme

Most authors stock their books with a combination of large and small messages. A large one might be "Take care of the rainforest"; a small one might "Never leave home without a flashlight." Copy the umbrella graphic organizer onto a sheet of paper. Write the story's biggest message on the brim and some of the smaller messages underneath it. Better hurry, though—it looks like rain!

The Great Gilly Hopkins by Katherine Paterson

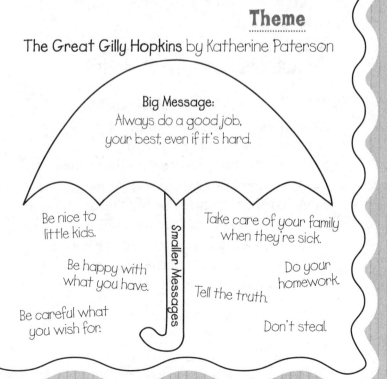

Big Message:
Always do a good job,
your best, even if it's hard.

Be nice to little kids.

Be happy with what you have.

Be careful what you wish for.

Smaller Messages

Take care of your family when they're sick.

Do your homework.

Tell the truth.

Don't steal.

CARD #51

Agree to Disagree

Do you agree with every single message in the book you just read? If not, choose one you "quibble" (disagree) with and write a paragraph supporting your viewpoint. If you like, share your opinion with a classmate who's read the same story. Does he or she side with you or the author? Discuss your ideas.

CARD #52

Pieces of the Pie

Time to roll up your sleeves and make a pie—a pie chart, that is! Draw a circle like the one at right. Then divide it into slices that illustrate the key themes—or ideas—of your book. (Draw big slices for big ideas and smaller slices for small ideas.) When you're done, swap "pies" with a friend who's completed the assignment and sample each other's results.

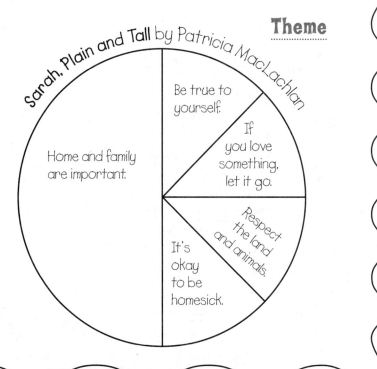

Sarah, Plain and Tall by Patricia MacLachlan

Be true to yourself.

If you love something, let it go.

Home and family are important.

Respect the land and animals.

It's okay to be homesick.

CARD #53

Story Flag

Celebrate the greatness of the book you just read by creating a commemorative flag! Take a look at some state and country flags for inspiration. Then use a sheet of paper and markers, crayons, or colored pencils to design your own. There are just two rules: be sure to include symbolic pictures and at least one symbolic color. (For example, if the story takes place in the Arctic, you might choose white to represent all the snow.) When you're done drawing, tape your story flag to a straw and wave it with pride!

⭐ **BONUS** ⁂⋯⋯⋯⋯⋯⋯⋯⋯⋯⋯⋯⋯⋯⋯⋯⋯⋯⋯⋯⋯⋯

For an extra challenge, write a paragraph explaining your choices.

CARD #54

Message in a Bottle

What is the main message of the book you just read? That grownups make mistakes, too? That bear cubs belong in the forest, not bathtubs? That honesty is always the best policy? Think carefully about the story. Then draw a bottle like the one at right

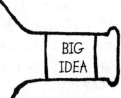

The theme of *Freaky Friday* is that you don't know about someone else's life until you spend a day living it. Plus, parents have a hard job.

BIG IDEA

Freaky Friday by Mary Rodgers

and fill it with the big idea. When you're finished, exchange your message in a bottle with a classmate who's read the same book. Compare your responses.

CARD #55

Theme

Seeing Double

Time to do a double take. Can you think of another book that has the same basic theme as the one you just finished? If so, copy the eyeglasses graphic organizer onto a sheet of paper and fill each "lens" with a book title and theme (as shown). Next, write a paragraph that compares the two books in more detail. How are they the same? How are they different?

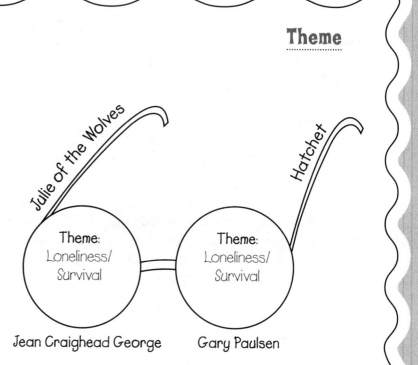

Julie of the Wolves

Hatchet

Theme: Loneliness/ Survival

Theme: Loneliness/ Survival

Jean Craighead George

Gary Paulsen

CARD #56

Theme

Skywriting

Does your book have a special theme or message that you'd like to share with the world...or at least your classmates? Write it in "skywriting" (like the example to the right). Then write a paragraph telling why you think it's important to spread the word far and wide.

In the Year of the Boar and Jackie Robinson
by Bette Bao Lord

100 Awesome Writing Prompts to Use With Any Book! © 2010 by Liza Charlesworth. Scholastic Teaching Resources

CARD #57

Five Senses Search

A skillful writer takes advantage of the five senses to bring a story to life. For example, he or she might set a scene by describing the sweet, sugary smell of a bakery or the squishy sensation of sticking one's fingers into a big bowl of chocolate icing. Give yourself ten minutes to search through your book and collect as many sentences as you can find that relate to each of the senses at right. Copy them onto a sheet of paper. Which sense did the writer rely on the most? The least? Which was your very favorite? Write about it!

1. Sight	4. Taste
2. Smell	5. Hearing
3. Touch	

CARD #58

Stand-Out Sentences

Q. How do talented authors resemble architects? **A.** They are able to craft great books from the building blocks of great sentences. Browse through your book and find three favorite sentences and copy them onto a building-block graphic organizer like the one at right. What makes them so great? Are they funny? Do they sound like poetry? Do they use cool metaphors? Write a paragraph that tells what you admire about each one and the author's writing style in general.

"So while you're telling her this sad, beautiful love story, and you're saying everything you feel—but everything— she's listening so hard you feel she's curled up inside your own head." PAGE 116

1

"She had long hair, the color of warm honey in the winter, the color of evening sunlight in the summer." PAGE 118

2

"The pie was cut and scoops of ice cream put on top of the flaky brown crust." PAGE 160

3

Dicey's Song by Cynthia Voigt

CARD #59

Writing Style

Quoting Characters

Dialogue is a tool good writers take advantage of to help move the story along and to provide important hints about a character's personality. Select a telling quote from the book you just read and copy it inside a speech balloon. What did that statement teach you about its speaker? Write your ideas in a thought bubble like the one at right. If you're feeling artistic, add cartoon drawings of that character and yourself.

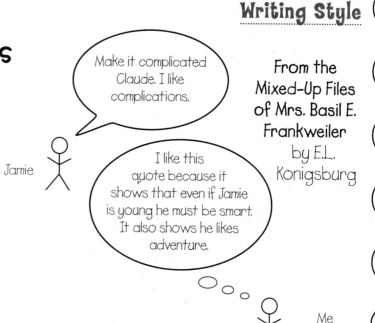

From the Mixed-Up Files of Mrs. Basil E. Frankweiler by E.L. Konigsburg

CARD #60

Writing Style

Simile Race

A lot of authors choose to spice up their writing with similes. A simile is a descriptive phrase that compares two seemingly unlike things with the connecting word *like* or *as*. Here are some examples:

- eyes blue *as* robins' eggs
- slow *as* molasses
- a grin *like* the Grand Canyon
- quick *like* a bunny

Get the idea? Good! Now copy a T-chart onto a sheet of paper, labeling one side "as" and the other "like." Then set a timer for ten minutes and race a classmate to see who can find and record the most similes from your book. No doubt the winner will be happy *as* a clam!

BONUS
For an extra challenge, try your hand at creating some sensational similes of your own!

CARD #61

Story Sleuth

Foreshadowing is when a writer leaves little clues to warn the reader about a dramatic event that will happen later in the story. For example, if a character has the sniffles on page 22 and a full-blown cold on page 56, the sniffles *foreshadowed* the cold. Copy the magnifying-glass graphic organizer onto a sheet of paper. Then play detective by searching through your book for an example of foreshadowing. Write the clue you found in the top half of the magnifying glass and write the important event it foretold in the bottom half. When you're done, compare your sleuthing with a friend who's read the same book. Did he or she find something different?

Clue:
Phillip's head hurts.
–page 13

Event:
Phillip is going blind.
–page 47

The Cay by Theodore Taylor

CARD #62

Time Travel

A *flashback* is when the author interrupts the telling of the story to describe an important event that took place in the character's past. For example, a book might be about the adventures of a girl and her pet gerbil—then BOOM!—suddenly the tale goes back in time to describe the day she received the gerbil as a gift from Aunt Lou. Browse through your book and see if you can find an example of flashback. (**Hint:** A flashback could take up a paragraph, an entire chapter, or more.) Did you find one? Great! Describe it inside the flashback arrow. Why do you think the author decided to use flashback? How did it help tell the story? Put your ideas in writing.

Holes by Louis Sachar

The boys ask why Stanley was sent to the work camp. He says he stole a pair of sneakers. Later tossing in bed—BOOM!—He's back in school. After being bullied by Derrick Dunne, Stanley rushed home, the sneakers fell from the sky and hit him on the head.

CARD #63

Writing Style

Box of Chocolates

A good book is a bit like a box of chocolates! How? Both are chock-full of delicious treats! A candy box might have chewy caramels, crunchy toffee, and gooey pecan clusters; a book might have inspiring characters, sensational similes, and fantastic flashbacks. Get the idea? Copy the chocolate box onto a sheet of paper. Then fill it with nine things you really liked about the author's writing style. When you are done, keep it handy to help "sweeten" your own writing!

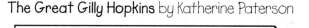

The Great Gilly Hopkins by Katherine Paterson

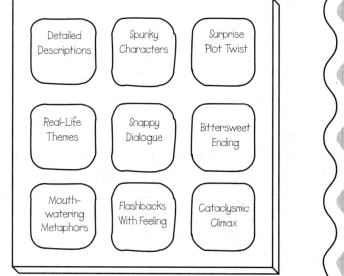

Detailed Descriptions	Spunky Characters	Surprise Plot Twist
Real-Life Themes	Snappy Dialogue	Bittersweet Ending
Mouth-watering Metaphors	Flashbacks With Feeling	Cataclysmic Climax

CARD #64

Writing Style

"A" Is for Awesome

F inally, your chance to fill in a report card...for the book you just read! Copy the seven categories onto a sheet of paper. Then give the author a grade for each item (A = Awesome, P = Pretty Good, S = So-so, and D = Disappointing). Be fair and be sure to include a sentence that explains your reasoning.

Report Card for

_____ (author's name) for

_____ (title of book)

1. Title:	Grade ____	Comments: _____
2. Characters:	Grade ____	Comments: _____
3. Plot:	Grade ____	Comments: _____
4. Settings:	Grade ____	Comments: _____
5. Theme:	Grade ____	Comments: _____
6. Dialogue:	Grade ____	Comments: _____
7. Language:	Grade ____	Comments: _____
8. Originality:	Grade ____	Comments: _____

CARD #65

Name That Genre!

Genre is just a fancy way of saying "type of book." Scan the list of genres at right and find the label that best describes the book you just read. Why do you think it fits into this category? Is this a genre that you like or don't like? Have you read other books in this category? Write all about it!

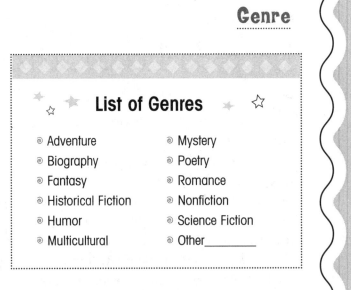

List of Genres

- Adventure
- Biography
- Fantasy
- Historical Fiction
- Humor
- Multicultural

- Mystery
- Poetry
- Romance
- Nonfiction
- Science Fiction
- Other_____

CARD #66

Genre Collage

Ready, set, get creative! Clip pictures and words from magazines that relate to the genre of your book. Then use them to make a cool collage.

CARD #67

Loop-de-Loop Comparisons

Have you read another book that shares the same genre as the one you are reading now? If so, rev up your engine to do this speedy comparison! Copy the loop-de-loop graphic organizer onto a sheet of paper, labeling the left side with the name of your new book and the right side with the name of a book you've read in the past. Inside each circle, write a mini-description of the plot. On the car, write the genre both share.

The Giver
by Lois Lowry

Among the Hidden
by Margaret Peterson Haddix

Jonas is made the receiver of memory by a futuristic society. At the end he runs away to change the future.

Luke is a hidden third child in a futuristic society. In the end, he must run away and risk everything to change lives for the other third children, like him.

Science Fiction

CARD #68

From Me to You!

If you had to recommend the book you're reading to a single classmate, who would it be? Mark? Maryanne? Monique? Use an index card to design a gift tag like the one at right, being sure to fill in all the requested info. When you're finished, attach your tag to the book with yarn and present it to that special someone!

To: Joe
From: Jesse

Title: The Adventures of Tom Sawyer
Author: Mark Twain

Genre: Adventure
Why the book is perfect for you: I thought you might like this because it's about a great guy who sometimes gets in trouble.

CARD #69

Genre Pennants

Three cheers for the book you just read! Design a genre pennant by writing your book's title plus its genre on a triangular shape like the one below. Next, challenge yourself to incorporate a symbol that really represents that genre. For example, you might choose a magnifying glass for a mystery novel or a clown for a humorous tale. What color should your flag be? Choose one that makes sense. When your work of art is done, write a paragraph that explains your choices.

CARD #70

That Reminds Me of a Movie

Mystery! Action-Adventure! Romance! Cat Comedy! Like books, movies have genres, too. Have you seen a film that shares the same genre as the book you are reading? If so, you are eligible to compare and contrast the two in writing. How are they the same? How are they different? Which did you prefer? Put your opinions into a paragraph.

CARD #71

Vocabulary Development

What a Word!

Did the book you're reading lead you to discover a new word that you truly treasure? Copy the treasure-chest graphic organizer onto a sheet of paper. On the inside, write a word that you love and its definition; on the outside, write why it's so precious to you. (**Hint:** Some comments you might include are: what the word added to the story, what the word reminds you of, how the word sounds, how you will make use of the word in your writing, etc.)

⭐ **Bonus** ....
For an extra challenge, use the fabulous new word in three sentences.

> ### The *Summer of the Swans*
> by Betsy Byars
>
> Kaleidoscope
>
> I like this word because I think kaleidoscopes are amazing. Inside are tiny pieces of glass and glitter that make magical patterns. Even though Sara's life is mixed up, it's also beautiful just like a kaleidoscope.

CARD #72

Vocabulary Development

Fictionary Definitions

In the mood for a little challenge? Try this! Hunt through your book and find a big word that's new to you. Read the sentence it's in. Read the paragraph that sentence is in. Now write the word on a sheet of paper and create a "fictionary" definition based on your best guess of its true meaning. (Be sure to guess the word's part of speech, too: verb, noun, adjective, etc.) When you've finished, look up the real definition and record it next to the fake one. Whether you were right, wrong, or in-between—congratulations! You just added a new word to your vocabulary.

100 Awesome Writing Prompts to Use With Any Book! © 2010 by Liza Charlesworth, Scholastic Teaching Resources

CARD #73

Synonym Banks

Synonyms are a collection of words that mean about the same thing. Browse through your book and find a word that's a great way of saying something simple (like *uttered* for "said" or *stunning* for "pretty"). Copy the piggy bank onto a sheet of paper and write that word in its coin slot. Next, challenge yourself to fill the bank with as many words as you can think of that have the same basic meaning. When you have finished, dip into your "bank" to inspire your own writing!

GROUCHY

sour	cranky	pensive
wicked	moody	sulky
testy	ornery	

Roll of Thunder, Hear My Cry
by Mildred D. Taylor

CARD #74

Antonyms Hunt

Antonyms are two words that have opposite meanings like *up* and *down,* or *black* and *white.* Got it? Good! Now crack open your book, take ten minutes, and challenge yourself to locate at least one antonym for each of the words at right. Record your finds on a sheet of paper. Ready, set, race!

1. Pretty	6. Ugly
2. Big	7. Small
3. Noisy	8. Quiet
4. Nice	9. Mean
5. Happy	10. Sad

100 Awesome Writing Prompts to Use With Any Book! © 2010 by Liza Charlesworth, Scholastic Teaching Resources

CARD #75

Three-Ring Sentences

When you encounter a lot of words you don't know, reading can become a bit of a three-ring circus. That why it's a smart idea to set aside a little time to tackle their meaning once and for all. Open your book, locate three new words, and write them on each ring as shown. Now use context clues and/or the dictionary to arrive at their correct definitions. When you do, use each in an original sentence, written in the appropriate ring. Assignment completed? Give yourself a round of applause.

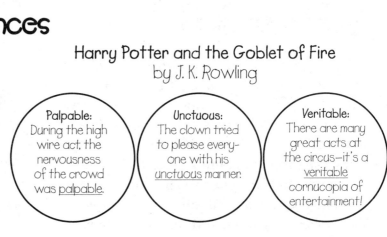

Harry Potter and the Goblet of Fire
by J. K. Rowling

Palpable: During the high wire act, the nervousness of the crowd was palpable.

Unctuous: The clown tried to please every-one with his unctuous manner.

Veritable: There are many great acts at the circus—it's a veritable cornucopia of entertainment!

CARD #76

Vocabulary Ladder

Get climbing and boost that vocabulary! Draw a ladder like the one at right on a sheet of paper. Now start to read your book. Every time you encounter a new word, add it to a rung. If it's a word you need to know to understand the story, stop and use context clues and/or the dictionary to figure out its meaning; write the definition under the step as shown. Otherwise, look it or them up after you are through reading for the day and record the definitions then. (**Hint:** If you fill up one ladder, just start a new one.)

Maniac Magee
by Jerry Spinelli

Trestle

A framework composed of vertical, slanted supports and horizontal crosspieces holding up a bridge.

Musicale

A social gathering at which a program of music is performed.

CARD #77

Mirror, Mirror

Mirror, mirror on the wall...who resembles *you* most of all? Choose the character from your book who is the most like you. Then use the graphic organizer like the one at right to record at least four ways his or her life *mirrors* your own. Do you both have red hair? Are you both a bit shy? Are the two of you really great at soccer? Take a good long look at yourself and write about it!

Personal Connections

Harry Potter and the Prisoner of Azkaban

1. She is very smart.
2. Her best friends are boys.
3. She gets picked on at school.
4. She is a loyal friend.

by J.K. Rowling

Hermione Granger

CARD #78

Apples and Oranges

Are you and one of the main characters in your book as different as apples and oranges? Copy the graphic organizer at right onto a sheet of paper. Label the apple with that character's name and fill it with a mini-description of him or her. Next, label the orange with *your* name and fill it with a mini-description of you. Even though you are very different, do you think the two of you could get along? Write a paragraph telling why...or why not!

Personal Connections

The Great Gilly Hopkins
by Katherine Paterson

Gilly is tough and can fight boys. Sometimes she is mean and sometimes she lies.

I am always honest and have never been in a fight in my life. Gilly would eat me for lunch!

Gilly Hopkins

Janet Watson

CARD #79

CD Soundtrack

Ready, set, rock! Pretend you're a rock star hired to create a soundtrack CD based on your book. Dig deep into your imagination and come up with the titles of 10 real or pretend tunes that capture feelings and events from the start of the story to the finish. Next, tell what you would name your CD and why.

★ **BONUS** ────────────────────────

For an extra challenge, design an awesome cover, too.

CARD #80

Personal Connections

Get in Shape!

Quick, if you had to pick one of the shapes at right to represent the story you just read, which would it be? A triangle because it's about three best friends? A diamond because the most important scene takes place at a baseball game? A circle because the main character ends up back where he started? Dig deep into your imagination and tell why the shape you selected reminds you of the story.

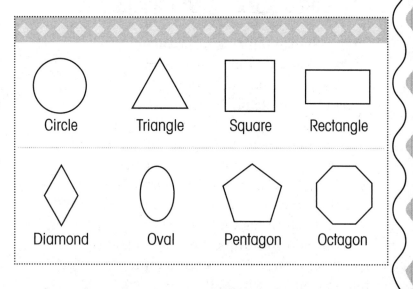

Circle   Triangle   Square   Rectangle

Diamond   Oval   Pentagon   Octagon

100 Awesome Writing Prompts to Use With Any Book! © 2010 by Liza Charlesworth. Scholastic Teaching Resources

CARD #81

Talk-Show Time

Pretend you're a talk-show host on a program called "Book Break" and you're interviewing a fascinating character from the story you've just read. First, write five meaningful questions you'd like to ask him or her. Next, switch seats and pretend you are that character. How would he or she respond? Think carefully and craft some great answers. Don't let your fans down!

CARD #82

E-Mail a Character

Did someone in the book you are reading make a choice that you just don't agree with? First, make up the perfect e-mail address for that character. Next, compose a pretend message explaining why you believe that decision was wrong and what action could have been taken instead. Do you think that character would agree with you or try to defend his or her choice? Get inside that character's head and write his or her e-mail response back to you. Keep the cyber chat going as long as you like.

CARD #83

Words of Wisdom

Did one of the characters in your book say something so insightful it really made you think? Copy those words of wisdom onto a fortune cookie slip like the one at right (making sure to credit the speaker). Then write about why the statement is so meaningful to you. When you're done, swap slips with a group of classmates and discuss. Do you all agree that these are words to live by?

"You don't go reaching out with your hand closed up." Gram –page 129

Dicey's Song by Cynthia Voigt

CARD #84

Star Search

Hooray for Hollywood! Imagine your book is being turned into a blockbuster movie and you've been hired to cast the lead role. Who would you pick and why? The person could be famous or someone you know from real life. Be sure to give at least three reasons why they'd be absolutely perfect for the part.

CARD #85

Personal Connections

That's a Keeper

Ten years from now what do you think you'll remember about the book you just read? That the settings were so real you saw pictures in your mind? That the main character reminded you exactly of your big brother? That one scene made you laugh so hard you fell off your chair? Think about it. Then copy the keepsake box onto a sheet of paper and fill it with your fondest memory.

Sarah, Plain and Tall
by Patricia MacLachlan

I will always remember when Sarah brushed Anna's hair and she felt like she had a mother again. My mom sometimes brushes my hair like that.

CARD #86

Personal Connections

The Problem Is...

No story or life is without conflict. Choose a problem from your book that is similar to a problem you've faced in real life. Describe both. How did the character's solution compare to your own? Write about it.

CARD #87

Framing the Story

A new museum is opening that tells all about the book you just read, and you've been hired to create the artwork! There's only one catch—instead of paints, you'll be using words. Label a big piece of paper "The Museum of _____" (the name of your book). Then draw six fancy frames, labeling them: main character, setting, plot, theme, genre, and writing style. Now it's time to fill each with a thoughtful description. When you're finished, invite classmates to "tour" the museum and share their comments.

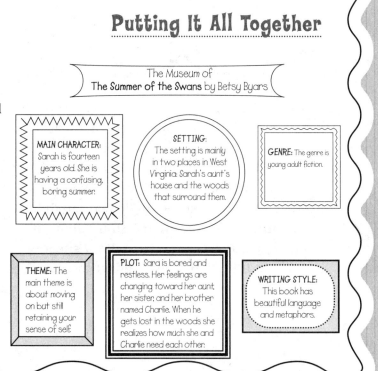

The Museum of
The Summer of the Swans by Betsy Byars

MAIN CHARACTER: Sarah is fourteen years old. She is having a confusing, boring summer.

SETTING: The setting is mainly in two places in West Virginia: Sarah's aunt's house and the woods that surround them.

GENRE: The genre is young adult fiction.

THEME: The main theme is about moving on but still retaining your sense of self.

PLOT: Sara is bored and restless. Her feelings are changing toward her aunt, her sister, and her brother named Charlie. When he gets lost in the woods she realizes how much she and Charlie need each other.

WRITING STYLE: This book has beautiful language and metaphors.

CARD #88

Book-Jacket Blurb

Did you flip for a recent book? If so, spread the word by writing a book jacket blurb that convinces others to read it, too. First, check out some jacket copy on real books to use as models. Then compose a few paragraphs that really sell it to your classmates. Be sure to include an exciting snippet of the plot and lots of thrilling adjectives.

★ **BONUS**

Use craft paper to design a new cover complete with jacket copy to slip on the actual book. On the back cover, you can even include pretend quotes—called "testimonials"—from famous folks, such as "*Hatchet* was so exciting, I called in sick to work just to finish it." —Superman

MARY POPPINS by P. L. TRAVERS

CARD #89

Critic's Corner

Pretend you're the brand-new critic for the *Literature-Lover Times*. What do you want readers to know about the book you just read? Write a cool column that includes information about the plot, genre, the things you liked and didn't like about the story, what it reminded you of, how it made you feel, and more. Would you recommend it others? Give it a rating of one to five stars. When you're finished, be sure to share your opinions with classmates.

CARD #90

I Love It, I Love It Not

Now that you've finished the book, are there some things that you loved about it...and some things you didn't love? Draw a daisy like the one at right and write the title of the book and the author on the leaves. Then, alternate writing things that were good about the story with things that were not so good in the petals (as shown at right). In the end, would you give the book a "green"-thumbs up or down? Tell why.

I like Claudia because she's smart.

I didn't like that the book had to end.

I didn't like that it took so long to find out why she ran away.

I like the surprise twist at the end.

I like Jamie because he's funny and loyal.

I didn't like that Mrs. Frankweiler took so long to solve the mystery.

I liked the mystery of the angel.

I didn't like the museum because it's scary at night.

From the Mixed-Up Files of Mrs. Basil E. Frankweiler

by E. L. Konigsburg

CARD #91

Creative Collage

Are you "scrappy"? Great! Then create a cool collage that tells all about your book! Turn on your imagination. Then use a stack of magazines to cut captions, words, photos, and illustrations that relate to the plot, characters, and settings plus your own feelings about the story. Arrange them on a sheet of paper. When your work of art is complete, write a few paragraphs that explain some of your choices.

CARD #92

Sensational Sequel

Pretend you've been hired to write a sequel to the book you just read. Think it through, then write a description of what you'd have happen in the follow-up story. When you're finished, swap story plans with a classmate who's done the same assignment. How do they compare? If you like, combine your ideas for the most sensational sequel of all time.

CARD #93

Character Trading Cards

Show what you know about the book you just read with this creative project! Use blank index cards to create a set of trading cards—one for each main character in the story. On the front, draw a picture of them and write their name. On the back, provide a description of their personality and appearance, plus fun facts such as their nickname, favorite food, or most embarrassing moment. When you're done, swap cards with classmates.

CARD #94

Stamp of Approval

The U.S. Post Office is creating a brand-new stamp to honor the book you just read and you've been selected to design it! On a piece of paper, sketch a super stamp that tells all about the book in pictures and symbols. When your work of art is complete, write a paragraph that explains your choices.

THAT'S A WRAP

CARD #95

Triple Scoop

Putting It All Together

Celebrate the book you just finished with a triple scoop! Copy the ice-cream graphic organizer onto a sheet of paper. Then, use it for a mini-retelling by writing a short description of the beginning, middle, and end in the three scoops as shown. The book's title and author go in the cone, and the genre inside the cherry. Now you better get started before it melts!

Fiction

BEGINNING: Andrew wants freckles like Nicky Lane's.

MIDDLE: Sharon gives him a recipe for freckle juice. Andrew makes and drinks it.

END: The juice doesn't work. Andrew draws blue freckles, then learns to be happy the way he is.

Freckle Juice
by
Judy Blume

CARD #96

Top-Ten List

Putting It All Together

What were the top-ten things that you liked best about the book you just finished? Create a list. Then share it with friends who haven't read the story. Bet they'll be itching to now!

CARD #97

Radio Ad

Was the story you just read totally awesome? If so, create a radio ad to sell your classmates on it. First, write a script that sings the book's praises and gives away just enough of a plot. (**Hint:** Be sure to use lots of exciting descriptions like *stupendous, thrilling,* and *utterly incredible*). After the writing is complete, make an audio recording. If you like, use funny voices and sound effects to grab listeners' attention. When you're happy with the finished product, share it with everyone. Did you make any sales?

The spine-tingling mystery that's taking 5th graders by storm...

CARD #98

Story Carpet

Honor the book you just read by designing a story carpet! Here's how: Copy the rug template like the one at right onto a sheet of paper. In the outside rectangle, create a pattern that tells something about the book's setting. (For example, if the story took place in Hawaii, you might incorporate a palm tree and shells.) In the middle rectangle, create a pattern that tells something about the main character. (For example, if she was great at sports, you might incorporate soccer balls and softballs.) In the center rectangle, draw your very favorite scene. (**Tip:** Close your eyes, then capture what you see in a sketch.)

Little Red Riding Hood

CARD #99

Wormy Awards

Pay tribute to your book's amazing cast of characters by hosting your own Wormy Awards! Decide which person should get each Bookworm Award and why. Be sure to justify your choices in writing. **Rules:** Awards can be given to the same character more than once. Categories can be skipped if no one fits the bill. Acceptance speeches are optional.

- Best Hero
- Best Villain
- Funniest Character
- Most Real Character
- Most Changed Character

- Most Adventurous Character
- Best Character in a Supporting Role
- Character Who Made the Most Mistakes
- Character Whom You'd Like to Be Friends With
- Character Whom You Would Not Want to Be Friends With

CARD #100

Time Capsule

Quick! What ten items would you put in a time capsule to represent the book you just read? A paintbrush because the main character is a talented artist? A feather because she wants to be a pilot? Make a list of your top ten picks. Be sure to include a sentence that explains each selection.